Lorikeet's Garden Breakfast

Written by: Jan Hill
Illustrations by: Lillian Falzon

Lorikeet's Garden Breakfast
Copyright © 2024 by Jan Hill
Website: www.jan-hill-books.com
Illustrator: Lillian Falzon

All rights reserved. No part of this publication may be reproduced, distributed, or transmitted in any form or by any means, including photocopying, recording, or other electronic or mechanical methods, without the prior written permission of the author, except in the case of brief quotations embodied in critical reviews and certain other non-commercial uses permitted by copyright law.

Tellwell Talent
www.tellwell.ca

ISBN
978-0-2288-1112-1 (Paperback)
978-0-2288-0314-0 (eBook)

Rainbow Lorikeets are so full of life, I find myself captivated by their fun-loving, mischievous nature.

This story, the first in a series for young readers is based on a family of Lorikeets who often visited my garden, bringing with them an abundance of pizazz and personality.

I hope through my words and the creative vision of Lillian Falzon, whose illustrations brought these characters to life, you enjoy a peek into the life of this colourful and quirky family.

It's early in the morning, the sun is just starting to rise over the hill and the sun's rays are creeping slowly through the trees.

In the forest it is quiet and peaceful, a gentle breeze is blowing through the tree tops with a few old leaves fluttering to the ground.

Lawrence, the Rainbow Lorikeet is awake and dressed in a brilliant green cloak which is lined with red and has a pastel green collar.

He wears a blue cap and a yellow and red vest. He prefers to be called Lawrence because he believes Larry doesn't give other birds the impression he is a mature Lorikeet with a family.

Lawrence sees his family are beginning to wake up and knows they will soon want breakfast.

Lawrence flies from the tree where his family are nesting to search the forest and nearby gardens for food. He flies over the same area he is familiar with, not too far from his family.

Lawrence scans for trees in blossom when he notices in a garden below there are some trays on old tree stumps and a human is putting seeds in the trays.

He perches high in a tree nearby checking the safety of the garden.

After a while Lawrence sees no danger in the garden and flies back to the nest, lets out several loud screeches calling his family and then takes off again in the direction of the garden.

Loretta, his life partner follows leading the children: Laura, Lance, Leroy, Lana, Lolita, and the youngest of the family, Loren and Lawrence Jnr (Larry).

As the Lorikeets have only perched in trees to feed, at first they fly over, under and next to the trays, awkwardly landing in the bushes or trees close by.

After several attempts, the Lorikeets finally judge the distance and land on the tray's edge and hold on tight. Because the chicks are only used to eating nectar from blossoms, at first they play with the seeds not knowing what to do with them.

They soon learn by watching their mother Loretta who picks up a seed, splits it open and eats the juicy flesh from the inside.

The chicks are so excited, they screech, chatter and sing, making so much noise that other families of Lorikeets in the neighbourhood hear them and before long several Rainbow Lorikeet families fly in, see the trays of seeds and join them for breakfast.

The Lorikeet families are happy to share the feast together and up to twelve Lorikeets sit on a tray taking turns of eating the juicy seeds, chirping to one another and watching around the garden to see what mischief they can get in to.

Lawrence decides the chicks are too noisy and wants some privacy for himself and Loretta so demands they go to another tray.

Lawrence is a bossy Lorikeet, he stands tall, puffs out his colourful yellow and red chest and bites and screeches until he and Loretta are alone on the tray.

Lawrence turns to check the chicks have settled and are safely feeding before turning to eat with Loretta.

A family of Lorikeets try to muscle in on his tray and again Lawrence stands tall, puffs out his red and yellow chest and lurches at the intruders, giving them their marching orders whilst protecting Loretta and showing how brave he is.

The Lorikeet family reluctantly scatter to other trays, screeching their disapproval at Lawrence's bossy attitude.

Some fly on to the ground to feast on the seeds that have dropped. Many wait in pairs in the bushes and trees nearby, chatting and preening one another, patiently waiting for their turn on a tray as there aren't enough for everyone.

Lawrence is so bossy, he stands on the edge of the tray looking down, making sure no unwanted Lorikeets try to climb up from underneath him.

Every now and again the Lorikeets fly off for exercise, showing off their acrobatic skills, dodging and weaving in-between the trees at high speeds then return screeching, whistling and chattering, enjoying each other, the food and the fun.

As the sun starts to move overhead and is directly beaming on the trays, Lawrence decides it's time to leave.

He screeches loudly, summoning his family and within a moment they all take flight screeching and whistling, making a colourful display of green, red and yellow as they fly away into the distance.

The other families of Lorikeets also take flight, calling to one another on their departure.

With breakfast successfully complete, peace and quiet returns to the garden once again and only the rustling of leaves in the breeze can be heard.

www.ingramcontent.com/pod-product-compliance
Lightning Source LLC
LaVergne TN
LVHW071654060526
838200LV00029B/453